Retrieval of the Soul

by
Jason Harris

Conscious Dreams
PUBLISHING

Retrieval of the Soul

Copyright © 2024 Jason Harris

All rights reserved. No part of this publication may be produced, distributed, or transmitted in photocopying, recording, or other electronic or mechanical methods, any form or by any means, including without the prior written permission of the publisher, except in the case of brief quotations embodied in critical reviews and certain other non-commercial uses permitted by copyright law.

First Printed in United Kingdom 2024

Published by Conscious Dreams Publishing
www.consciousdreamspublishing.com

Edited by Elise Abram

Typeset by Oksana Kosovan

ISBN: 978-1-915522-56-6

Contents

- 5   Introduction
- 7   My Hearing Voices Experience
- 11   A Forensic Experience
- 15   Stigma
- 19   Imagine Feeling Lost
- 23   Anxiety
- 27   Gaining Strength Through Others
- 31   Learning to be Compassionate to Oneself
- 35   Changing Perspectives
- 39   Accepting a New Me
- 43   Forming a Positive Identity Statement
- 49   Trauma in the Body
- 53   Participation
- 57   You're a Ray of Sunshine. Live
- 61   The Lord is Merciful and True
- 65   Conclusion

Introduction

My name is Jason Harris. I volunteer as a peer tutor for the Recovery College in Norfolk, East Anglia, and I am currently working as a peer support worker for their Early Intervention Psychosis Team based in Norfolk. I also help facilitate the Hearing Voice Group in Norfolk. For those who may not be familiar with either of these titles, I am someone who shares their lived experience in the hope it may inspire others on their journeys to recovery.

I have experienced hearing voices for over ten years; some may be more familiar with the term auditory hallucinations. Voice hearing may be linked to psychosis, and a lot of people are unaware of what they should do when having these experiences. A lot of people report feeling alone when having this experience, and I still do from time to time. I have heard people report they feel isolated from the world, lost, misunderstood, not listened to, confused, and frightened. This is just a snippet of the things someone with these experiences may feel, but it's very individual, and people tend to interpret their experiences in different ways.

I started writing poetry about my experiences roughly five years ago, which was a good way for me to channel my thoughts, feelings, and emotions, as well as express myself. It was also another way to tell my story and hopefully encourage others.

I have found listening to others sharing their stories reassuring, refreshing, and inspiring. I have grown to be passionate about giving back — it's what drives and motivates me. In Recovery College, we look at an acronym called C.H.I.M.E, which stands for Connections, Hope, Identity, Meaning and Empowerment. This certainly gives me meaning and a purpose, and I enjoy supporting and helping others try to make sense of their situations.

My Hearing Voices Experience

My battle with hearing voices is ongoing and every day. This poem talks about some of the thoughts I have, how they make me feel, and the impact it has.

I always saw myself as a strong-minded individual who wasn't easily frightened, but this experience was so overwhelming that it brought me to a state of fear. I found it confusing that only I could hear these voices, and it was hard to comprehend why I was unable to see the speakers. It wore me down over time, causing me to feel defenceless and as if I had no option but to flee to different parts of the country and abroad until I eventually ended up in hospital, where I would remain for two years.

I felt alone with my experience at the time, and hearing other stories in a similar vein was helpful and inspiring. It helped me see how powerful sharing and talking with the right people can be and led me to think about different ways I could also share my story, bringing a message of hope while helping others to see they're not alone.

My Hearing Voices Experience

I have spent a lot of time wishing
Things were different
And so many days being bedridden
I used to be confident; some would say outspoken
Now I feel lonely, frightened and broken
I have gone from stable to feeling unable
Having an identity to just a label
My diagnosis has become my name
And it has left me feeling ashamed and afraid
Also, mentally and physically drained
Wishing someone or something would
come to my aid
seeking knowledge
That might ease my fears and make me
less worried
Up till this point, it has been nothing but horrid
Each and every day, all I can hear are critics
Bottled emotions have dampened my spirit
Smiling and stating, "Everything is fine"
To avoid addressing what's truly inside
Feeling like an outcast, not knowing where you fit
Wishing my experience
Was like a broken leg with a chance of being fixed
You see, a lot of the years, I have just
been listening
An outsider might say his voices have
imprisoned him
But "sharing is caring," like my
daughter would say
For those who can relate
I hope this might encourage you to do the same
through sharing, we hope to see we're not alone

And inspire each other to achieve our goals
Through others' stories, it has helped me to gained strength
Regardless of the height there is a way over the fence
I now take time to appreciate every step
And I now give thanks for every breath
I have learnt not to fight but accept
And I have learnt to love instead of neglect.

A Forensic Experience

Going into the hospital for the first time, I was anxious and not sure what to expect. I often heard people describing hospitals as a negative experience, which, for some, it probably is. For me, that wasn't the case. I managed to build some good relationships with staff and patients with whom I am still in contact to this day.

Although I didn't have as much access to my family as I would've liked, the relationships I managed to build felt like family in some ways as they helped me focus on the positives more than the negatives. It's easy to lose hope when going into hospital as you can become restricted in many ways, and I suppose it can lead to frustration.

The questions often being asked of me were how long I would be there, and how long would it take for me to recover? I also found myself asking the same questions. After spending two years in hospital, I was released back out into the community with a burning desire to share in the hope it would encourage others to keep faith in their recovery and that things can change.

A Forensic Experience

It's difficult because I am away from my family
But at least in here, people seem to understand me
When we talk, we often relate
And sometimes, joke about how we could escape

My voices and thoughts are like Formula 1 racing
Up and down this hallway, I am
constantly pacing
Not sure who to trust, so I'm anticipating
Just the not knowing is extremely frustrating

Scary to think this could be forever
Deep down, I am hoping that things get better
Burdened with guilt from an honest mistake
And all they can see is what my symptoms display

On paper, they get a bit of the story
I try to explain, but they seem to ignore me
It helps to keep busy throughout the day
Although they mean well, I dread CPA

What will they say? So many questions
Kick starts my anxiety and heightens my senses
I get really angry when people don't listen
Am in hospital, or am I in prison

Luckily, I have responded well to medication
And have been granted leave through hard work
and dedication
The light seemed dim, but now it's bright
So, try to keep faith, try not to lose sight

Stigma

There still seems to be stigma around psychosis, which can make it hard for some to open up about what they're experiencing.

For me, it had a lot to do with the fear of judgement and how I might be perceived by others close to me or in public. I have seen similar experiences portrayed in a negative light in the media and thought it better to remain silent, at least in the beginning. I thought it was a good way to cope, and it served a purpose for a while, but the longer it went on, the more draining it became as I had no outlet. It felt as if I was holding a dirty secret.

Whether it's our own stigma or the way others in society perceive us, it can add a lot of weight and increase the impact of what we're feeling. I have found it helpful to have conversations with people who can relate and whom I can trust.

Saying it's a stigma is a bias that shames us all.

Stigma

Stigma doesn't care who it hurts
It can be biased and devalue a person's worth
It will often leave you in the lurch
On your knees or on a search
Possibly to find a cure
Or something to help you feel reassured
It tends to leave its host floored
Feeling alone and unsure
Jumbled thoughts and mixed emotions reside
It like a disease that first attacks the mind
Slowly working its way to the eyes
Causing its victims to become blind
Casting an illusion over their lives
Not allowing outsiders to see inside
Steering up confusion and causing strife
Partly responsible for why there's a divide
Smart how it uses our fears to decide
Somehow intercepts the channel
From our hearts to our minds
It seems to feed off self-doubt
And manipulate what's perceived
For example, when you look at a homeless person
What is that you see?

Imagine Feeling Lost

After leaving hospital, I was unsure who I could trust in the community, especially now that I had a diagnosis.

Some of the people I spoke to weren't reassuring and left me in a state of limbo. I wasn't even sure who I was anymore. I was also worried about the nature of the illness and the stigma around it.

I didn't feel as if I would be accepted in society, and I felt alone, afraid and ashamed. It felt as if I was just existing rather than living, and although some people would take the time to listen, it still felt as if no one really understood what I was going through or how I truly felt. When I spoke with others in similar situations, they told me that they, too, felt the same. It was one of the reasons why I wanted to capture the essence of what I felt, like feeling lost.

Hopefully, this poem will help supporters, family members or friends to have some kind of idea of what some people might feel inside when experiencing the feeling of being lost, although this might not be the case for everyone as experiences can differ.

Imagine Feeling Lost

Imagine being dropped off in the mountains, not knowing what path to take

Imagine being a young child, left alone in an unfamiliar place

Imagine having a diagnosis that wasn't helpful in any way

Imagine feeling trapped, not knowing how to escape

Imagine being described as mentally insane

Imagine being told your life might never be the same

Imagine your neighbours deemed you unsafe

Imagine the people around that don't make you feel safe

Imagine having friends who can't understand your pain

Imagine being self-critical, thinking you're the one to blame

Imagine being unrecognisable despite having the same face

Imagine all the things you found meaningful slowly fading away

Imagine being in the world and feeling as if others are unable to relate

Now, imagine what that might feel like, and how you can make a change.

Anxiety

I didn't realise how badly anxiety can affect a person's wellbeing. Whether it's the thought of feeling close to death or feeling hopeless, the experience is real and can often be overlooked.

The feeling is not one that can be brushed off or thought away in a day. When on the other side I too thought: *surely you can just bring yourself out of it.* For some, it can be detrimental and wear a person down. Experiencing the attacks and seeing others having attacks, I can truly empathise.

My own experience was so overwhelming and made life very difficult for myself and others, and sometimes leading to isolation and frustration seeking answers as to why I feel this way.

I have found it helpful in the moment reciting bible verses and thinking of calming environments as well as talking myself through situations.

Anxiety

I'm about to leave the house
and my mood is bright
as I step outside
I notice that something's not right

My heart is racing
and so are my thoughts
My lungs feel blocked
I fear a storm

I start to question
If it's the end
So I think it wise
to call a friend

I can't get through
which then heightens the panic
I start to worry
and then become static

Desperate for help
but there's no one in sight
The sad thing is
It feels like I'm going to die

I'm slipping away
it becoming harder to breathe
As I'm saying my goodbyes
see how much life means

As I vision a happy place
It brings with it some ease
Which then calms the mind
and allows me to breathe

Gaining Strength Through Others

There are times we feel low and defeated and may need to draw on the strength of others.

This poem highlights the fact that situations can change almost instantly, sometimes without having a clear explanation, but having the right people around can help us to come out of it.

There have been many times in my journey when I hit a wall and was overwhelmed with doubt, fear and confusion, unsure if I would ever find my way out, but thankfully, I had people around me who cared and were willing to step in to help carry the load.

They did this by reassuring me, speaking positivity into my life, reminding me of my accomplishments and offering gentle encouragement.

Though it's nice to feel empowered, there is no harm in seeking help when you need it. Some may believe this is a weakness, but I don't believe it is. For me, it's a sign of strength.

There are always people who care and are willing to lend a hand for the right reasons.

Gaining Strength Through Others

All of a sudden there were some unexpected changes
Experiences beyond mine and others' imaginations
I was so desperate for an explanation
But instead I was left alone with tension and frustration

At first I tried to escape It
Try moving around only to find that
I couldn't shake It
Had never felt low and deflated
Even blamed myself for paths I had taken

I had lost all sight of hope or any aspirations
Couldn't see a future beyond my situation
For a while I was living in isolation
At this point it felt as if the stigma had infiltrated

But I came across peers who were an Inspiration
Which gave me the strength to be courageous
I still needed help from others and time to turn the pages
But just knowing I had a safe space to share was amazing

Learning to be Compassionate to Oneself

This poem is about having compassion towards myself and learning to be kind to myself, trying not to find fault or being self-critical despite my situation or any challenges I may face.

Some people find it easier to show compassion towards others yet difficult to show that same compassion towards themselves. When speaking with people, some of the reasons they mentioned were that I didn't deserve it, or it was probably Karma for what I had done in the past. Some saw it as being selfish or not wanting to be a burden to others.

This is something I found difficult, and it would occasionally leave me feeling quite drained and empty. After a while, it caused me to hit a block. There is a saying that you can't pour from an empty cup.

Over time, I have come to realise just how important it can be to compliment and treat yourself sometimes. Learning more about compassion has helped me view my experience and myself differently, rather than blame myself and get frustrated about all the things I think are not working or things I feel are wrong with me. I have learnt to appreciate my achievements, whether they are big or small, and to be grateful for the things I could be, acknowledge the positives within the day, and see my experience as a journey, bearing in mind that some days will be better than others. Being able to change perspectives has helped me move forward.

Learning to be Compassionate to Oneself

I was able to have compassion for others
But was harsh towards myself
I would often get upset
When I thought things weren't going well
I would blame and criticise
And that would impact my health
Till I realised acknowledging your achievements
Even if they are small may help
It can be helpful to take time out
To treat and pamper yourself
And although it may be tough
It's nice to enjoy the things we can as well
When our cups are empty
We can't pour for someone else
And applying too much pressure
Can sometimes set us up to fail
What a wonderful feeling when our kind deeds
help others to excel
But it's also important that we are kind to
ourselves

Changing Perspectives

This poem is about switching my focus to the road ahead and imagining what the journey could be like whilst trying not to let today's realities affect my future.

My mood was often low, and I was often self-critical. I had to learn to be compassionate with myself and allow myself time to heal. I found it helpful to note down my achievements, no matter how small, as it enabled me to see the positives in my journey and the possibility that things could change.

Rather than rushing the process, I tried to let nature take its course and not bombard myself with endless goals. I found it easier to go with the flow whilst trying new things along the way. This enabled me to develop new ideas and form new passions, which transformed my personality, adding some lovely new aspects to my identity.

Despite being faced with numerous challenges, I felt I somehow came out stronger.

Changing Perspective

Sometimes our thoughts can lead us to overthink
And bring what may not be a reality
into existence
The battle itself can break our resistance
while our experiences may cause us to see
ourselves different

For some it may come with a lot of pressure
And there may be people thinking it's easy to
get better
Accepting what's happening may take some time
 you're the best judge of how you feel inside

One thing to remember is that you're
still breathing
And where there's hope there is a chance
of healing
Try to note down the things you're achieving
and most importantly don't stop believing

Our journeys may require self-compassion
and patience
Can be useful at times not to have a destination
With changing perspective comes the realisation
that I am more than a diagnosis or one of
stigma's creations

Accepting a New Me

This poem is about how I found acceptance. It demonstrates how acceptance can be useful and how it has helped me in my journey.

Getting caught up in my battle with the voices stole my joy and identity. It also stole my ability to focus on other things. It took up a lot of my time and energy, which made it hard to engage in anything meaningful.

I attended a course called Act on Life, which got me thinking about acceptance and how acceptance can be helpful. In my case, it was about learning to accept the fact that I hear voices but not necessarily to accept the horrible things they were saying. I also attended another course called Living Well with Hearing Voices, which helped me to realise that voice hearing is more common than I previously thought. I also learnt that people heard voices for many different reasons, which, again, helped me realise that I wasn't weird or alone.

I began acknowledging other parts of my identity and challenging my experience in a more positive way. For example, I did not allow what I experienced to dictate my life or define me.

It helped free up my focus and allowed me to put my energy into meaningful things, things that gave me joy and purpose. It also allowed me the flexibility to explore new ideas whilst enabling me to build a life with which I was content.

Accepting a New Me

Acceptance can be hard for so many reasons
For some a diagnosis is not appealing
Getting caught in the battle can steal our freedom
and leave us feeling alone and defeated

Who wants to endure a life of treatment?
Being stigmatised by others or mistreated
It's a big choice and one that's not easy
and I needed time to actually see me

I realised that I was there underneath it all
How I live alongside it doesn't define me at all
How I see my future that's down to me
And I have learnt to appreciate that I am unique

As I grew in acceptance the more I felt free
Free to focus and able to breathe
Able to relax and able to see
that I am now free to explore a new me

Forming a Positive Identity Statement

This poem is about identity and how changing the way I saw myself helped make a difference, in my experience.

It can be easy to lose your identity, especially after being given a diagnosis with which you're not happy or you don't believe fits with your experience. For some, it can lead to believing their diagnosis defines them, which we know is not true. In fact, our identity is made up of a lot of different things that change over time.

There was a point at which I thought my experiences defined me, and I became blind to the various other parts of my identity that often made me ashamed and doubtful about the future.

I found myself buying into the different stigmas, forming a negative account of myself that wasn't helpful to me. Things slowly changed over time through discussions with peers and professionals, which helped me gain a better understanding of my identity and broaden my view, allowing me to see the positives.

I thought it would be good to write a statement as a personal reminder to stop myself from falling into those same old thought patterns, highlighting the different parts of my identity and the person I would like to be or see myself as.

Negative Identity

Why is this happening?
I'm ashamed of what I can become
It must be Karma
For something I have done
I feel worthless and stupid
That decision was so dumb
My diagnosis seems dangerous
Don't blame them for wanting to run
I don't deserve anything good
And I am a burden to everyone
Better to bottle my emotions
To the point where I feel numb
Just want to turn back the clock
Because this seems too difficult to overcome
I'm useless and weird
To others I'm no fun
I'm so overweight
Look at you, fat plum
What hurts the most
Is that I now believe I have become an
embarrassment to my mum

Positive Identity

I am a father
I am a giver
I am respectful and mindful of others
I am determined
I am a believer; my faith has seen me through many matters
I am creative
I am strong
I am patient
I am passionate
I am loving
I am caring
I am forgiving
I am compassionate
I am a child of God
I am fearfully and wonderfully made
I am trustworthy
I am servant
I am grateful for every day

Trauma in the Body

This poem is about trauma within our bodies and how we sometimes experience trauma without our minds knowing why and where it is coming from. As some may know, trauma is not just in our heads. It can also be stored in the body, and from time to time, it may be triggered for numerous reasons. We are not always given a clear explanation. We also know that it can have an impact on our health in future years.

Our bodies are clever, and through our senses, they seem able to detect and recognise past events. Although we may not remember, the body still seems to be able to remember, which is quite fascinating.

I have found it interesting in my own experiences not always being able to identify the cause, which often leaves me asking a lot of questions.

Trauma in the Body

I can smell the aroma of a time before
The body goes numb; it's like it's been here before
The mind starts racing
And in comes the pain
The body tenses up
And I start to feel the strain
It's like it's fighting something
But I am not quite sure
But it feels like the body's been here before

I start to feel breathless
And out of control of myself
My senses are responding
But I feel powerless within myself
I am screaming "Get a grip"
The body just ignores
It's like it's trying to warn me
That it's been here before

I'm looking back through my memory
Searching through my mind
I am making predictions
I am so ahead of time
Suddenly, I feel hot
It feels like my bones are cracking
I feel sadness
Like the body has remembered what happened

Participation

Participation and being a part of something can make you feel the impact it has. Participation can make a huge difference for some, and it's always lovely to see people connecting with others or the things they enjoy doing.

Developing psychosis was hard to take, and it was extremely hard to live with what I was experiencing. It hindered some of my relationships and made it nearly impossible to engage in most things that usually brought me joy. I spent six or seven years, at least, living in my own little bubble, where it felt safe. At times, I felt hopeless. I was often cautious of my surroundings. Other times, I gained an excessive amount of weight due to a lack of energy diet, exercise plus the medication was quite sedating. I truly missed playing football and hadn't kicked a ball competitively for 7 years one way to sum it up was I guess I felt trapped. Despite my situation, I often fantasise about playing football again, as it was one of my biggest passions, something I had been successful with over the years. I felt as if it had been stolen from me, and I was desperate for another opportunity.

After seven years of what I would call rehabilitation, I managed to shed some of the weight and was feeling better about myself.

Whilst out on a walk, I bumped into a neighbour, and after our conversation, after sharing our passion for football, he kindly helped me find a team. It felt amazing when I stepped out onto the pitch, the banter started, and I felt at home. It felt so good to be back doing something I loved and connecting with others.

It truly filled me with hope, as I thought I would have to live out the remainder of my days being miserable and in my little bubble. Luckily, that wasn't the case. Participating has helped me in a wide range of areas. Through participating, my confidence has grown, my connections have expanded, and so have my resources. It felt as If my life was starting to have some meaning and purpose again. Not only did others help me change my perspective, but it also challenged some of my own stigmas. I eventually opened up to some of the boys about my experience, and they did not treat me any differently from the other lads.

Participation

Participation has helped me to reconnect
And rediscover values in a time of neglect
I was feeling alone unsure and upset
Scared of the world not knowing what to expect

Trying to face the challenges on my own
But I was feeling so far away from my goals
I needed encouragement and others to
hold the hope
Participation has made me feel whole

I once felt like an outsider looking in
And that's because I thought I didn't fit in
Only to realise that was my perspective
And there were people out there who
were accepting

Having a safe space to talk and project in
Has helped to inspire hope and a sense
of direction
Through gaining confidence I've formed new
connections
Whilst also revisiting some old affections

You're a Ray of Sunshine. Live

This poem talks about a process that some may experience in their journeys. It is also about the richness that can come from that experience.

Recovery stories are powerful, and they can be used to shed light on others. It's also lovely to see or hear the victories in one's recovery, as it can help others to understand their own journeys better and spark hope in their recovery.

So many people feel isolated and alone, wondering If things will ever change — I certainly felt that way — but hearing others' recovery stories brought relief, hope and togetherness. Although people haven't experienced exactly what I did, there was empathy, understanding and encouragement as well, which helped me find the strength to move forward in my journey.

We are stronger than we may think or know
without tests we would never develop or grow
In life we may experience highs and lows
But when we overcome challenges, it can
give us hope

Flowers are beautiful just like you
and all have a process they must go through
But just like the sunlight that helps them to bloom
To a stranger or friend that could be me or you

So, let your light shine like the sun or the stars
although you may not believe it that's
what you are
A beacon of light in times when it's hard
A message of hope that may help change
someone's path

The Lord is Merciful and True

My faith has played a huge part in my journey, so this last poem is a tribute and testament to the Lord's love.

Being able to seek the Lord's guidance has taken me further than I could ever imagine. I was no saint. I have made mistakes and will still probably continue to do so. For me, it's normal, but what's more important to me is what I learn from them.

Despite all of my wrongs, I always felt the warmth of His presence, and I have felt highly favoured as He has stuck with me throughout my journey.

To be honest, at first, I wasn't sure why, but it became apparent that He is love itself. Although I don't deserve His blessing, I am truly grateful for all He has done. Therefore, it's only right He receives all the credit.

Thank you

God has been merciful
And having faith is better than any wand
Many times when I have felt weak
His words have kept me strong
Where there seemed to be no way
His light has always shone
He has opened my eyes and
enabled me to see beyond

God is always there
Not only when we're worried or afraid
He wants a relationship and can speak
in many ways
Faith as small as a mustard seed that's
what He says
The world may see our brokenness but what God
sees is great

So, thank you, Lord, for your love
And for helping me through the pain
The warmth of your presence has made
me feel safe
I was close to self-destruction but your word
kept me sane
Ever so grateful that I can call upon your name
(Jesus Christ)

Conclusion

I am aware there is still stigma out there, and that can sometimes make people fearful about opening up and sharing their experiences, whether it's our own stigma or the way others in society perceive us. I get that it's not an easy thing to do for some, and they may be able to open up and share their experiences safely with the people they trust.

There is still a long way to go, but it's nice to see that some things are changing, and more people are talking about it. I think it's important to normalise people's experiences and validate them, whether or not it fits with our own understanding or beliefs.

It's a nice feeling to be included rather than segregated. In one of my poems, I talk about participation and the positive effects connecting with someone or something can bring. I truly believe there is something magical and special about people coming together and helping each other to make sense of challenging situations.

On my journey, I found that having a combination of things, including support from others, has helped. It can be helpful to have a safe space where you can confide in others. This may be a useful way to release some of those bottled-up feelings or emotions that may be eating away at you.

Yet again, this might not be the case, as our experiences are individual. I personally had a bad experience, as my voices were very negative, and having that as an option was helpful.

This book was inspired by my real-life experiences.
Thank you for reading my book.
I hope it helps someone.

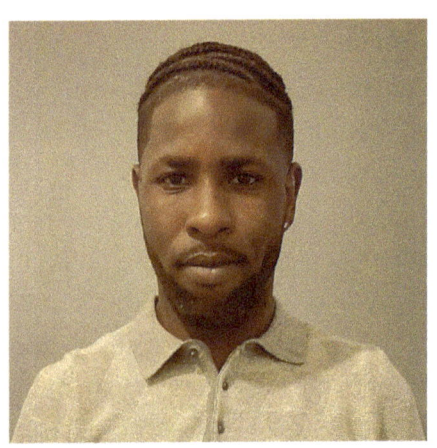

Jason Harris

Conscious Dreams
PUBLISHING

Transforming diverse writers
into successful published authors

www.consciousdreamspublishing.com

authors@consciousdreamspublishing.com

Let's connect

www.ingramcontent.com/pod-product-compliance
Lightning Source LLC
Chambersburg PA
CBHW041320110526
44591CB00021B/2848